Samuel French Acting Edition

An Evening of Culture
Faith County II: The Saga Continues

by Mark Landon Smith

SAMUELFRENCH.COM   SAMUELFRENCH.CO.UK

Copyright © 1994 by Mark Landon Smith
All Rights Reserved

AN EVENING OF CULTURE is fully protected under the copyright laws of the United States of America, the British Commonwealth, including Canada, and all other countries of the Copyright Union. All rights, including professional and amateur stage productions, recitation, lecturing, public reading, motion picture, radio broadcasting, television and the rights of translation into foreign languages are strictly reserved.

ISBN 978-0-874-40860-7

www.SamuelFrench.com
www.SamuelFrench.co.uk

For Production Enquiries

United States and Canada
Info@SamuelFrench.com
1-866-598-8449

United Kingdom and Europe
Plays@SamuelFrench.co.uk
020-7255-4302

Each title is subject to availability from Samuel French, depending upon country of performance. Please be aware that *AN EVENING OF CULTURE* may not be licensed by Samuel French in your territory. Professional and amateur producers should contact the nearest Samuel French office or licensing partner to verify availability.

CAUTION: Professional and amateur producers are hereby warned that *AN EVENING OF CULTURE* is subject to a licensing fee. Publication of this play(s) does not imply availability for performance. Both amateurs and professionals considering a production are strongly advised to apply to Samuel French before starting rehearsals, advertising, or booking a theatre. A licensing fee must be paid whether the title(s) is presented for charity or gain and whether or not admission is charged. Professional/Stock licensing fees are quoted upon application to Samuel French.

No one shall make any changes in this title(s) for the purpose of production. No part of this book may be reproduced, stored in a retrieval system, or transmitted in any form, by any means, now known or yet to be invented, including mechanical, electronic, photocopying, recording, videotaping, or otherwise, without the prior written permission of the publisher. No one shall upload this title(s), or part of this title(s), to any social media websites.

For all enquiries regarding motion picture, television, and other media rights, please contact Samuel French.

MUSIC USE NOTE

Licensees are solely responsible for obtaining formal written permission from copyright owners to use copyrighted music in the performance of this play and are strongly cautioned to do so. If no such permission is obtained by the licensee, then the licensee must use only original music that the licensee owns and controls. Licensees are solely responsible and liable for all music clearances and shall indemnify the copyright owners of the play(s) and their licensing agent, Samuel French, against any costs, expenses, losses and liabilities arising from the use of music by licensees. Please contact the appropriate music licensing authority in your territory for the rights to any incidental music.

IMPORTANT BILLING AND CREDIT REQUIREMENTS

If you have obtained performance rights to this title, please refer to your licensing agreement for important billing and credit requirements.

An Evening of Culture was first produced by the Hadwen Park Players, in Worcester, MA.. Directed by David Russell. The cast was as follows:

VIOLET FARKLE	Pam Mitchell
MILDRED CARSON	Denise Smith
DELBERT FINK	Dave Russell
FAYE MCFAYE	Cheryl Knapton
RUTHANN BARNS	Anne Nickerson
NAOMI CARSON	Debbie Kozik
LUTHER CARSON	Bob Engelke
BUBBA BEDFORD	Allan Moir

CHARACTERS

VIOLET FARKLE -- Naomi's pretty, sweet sister-in-law who is everyone's favorite and the only person in Mineola with any sense. She's the director of this evening's production. 20-ish.

MILDRED CARSON -- A middle-aged busy body who makes it her business to know everyone else's business and who won't hesitate for a moment to tell you what you should do, when you should do it and who it's to be done with. She has the female lead in this evening's presentation, a role she takes *very* seriously.

DELBERT FINK -- Local pig farmer and *Romeo and Juliet* set builder, neither of which he does very well. 30-ish. He also plays the role of the Prince in the second act.

FAYE McFAYE -- Flirty, young checker at the local A&P who has the hots for Delbert, who fails to return the sentiment. She plays the role of the Nurse. 20-ish.

RUTHANN BARNS -- Wife of the Reverand Ezekiel Barns, local Moral Majority leader, and President of the Mineola Council for Cultural Recognition. She plays the role of a Servant and the Friar. 40-ish.

NAOMI FARKLE CARSON -- Wife of Luther Carson, owner of The Bee-Luv-Lee Beauty Salon, and Mildred's best friend. She grudingly plays the role of Juliet's mother. 30 to 40-ish.

LUTHER CARSON -- Husband to Naomi, owner of "Luther's Lube 'n Tune", and Delbert's best friend who plays the role of Benvolio. 30 to 40-ish.

BUBBA BEDFORD -- Owner of "Bubba's Gas 'n Go" who's a bit simple minded and much to Mildred's consternation, plays the role of Romeo. 20 to 30-ish.

SETTING

The gynasium of the Mineola Magnet Middle School on the opening night of the Mineola Council for Cultural Recognition's production of Romeo and Juilet.

TIME

The present.

AUTHOR'S NOTE

It is imperative that these characters be played with the utmost sincerity. They're trying really hard to make this a good production, but it just isn't going to happen. Any indication by the actors as to the humor of the script will greatly weaken its credibility.

Dedication

To my beautiful and loving wife, Valerie, whom I adore, for her neverending encouragment, support and for sharing my life. ILYMTWCT.

To Mom, Dad, "Grams," and Mama and Daddy Jones - my dear family for their support and sharing my joy.

To all the fans of *Faith County* and the wonderful characters who live there. Thank you.

To a God of mercy and grace who gave me a second chance and a niche.

Mineola Council for Cultural Recognition
&
The Bee-Luv-Lee Beauty Salon
("on Main Street")
Present
Romeo and Juliet
by
Mr. Bill Shakespeare

Additional dialogue by Mrs. Naomi Louise Farkle Carson

Starring
Ruthann Barns Bubba Bedford Luther Carson Naomi Louise Farkle Carson Faye McFaye and Mildred Hayworth Carson as Juliet.

Directed by Violet Farkle
Sets Built by Delbert Fink
Make-up by Naomi Louise Farkle Carson

The Mineola Council for Cultural Recognition would like to thank Skeeter's Hay and Feed for providing the refreshments, The Happy Heifer Steakhouse for hosting the opening night festivities, Mrs. Norma Dodson for sewing the costumes, and the Mineola Magnet Middle School for the use of their facilities. Funding for this production has been made possible by Bubba's Gas 'n Go, Luther's Lube & Tune, the A&P, The Bee-Luv-Lee Beauty Salon and Fink Pink Pig Farms.

An Evening of Culture

FAITH COUNTY II:
The Saga Continues

ACT I SCENE 1

(SETTING: The Mineola Community Theatre, which is housed in the converted Mineola Magnet Middle School. It is opening night of the Mineola Council for Cultural Recognition's annual spring production. This year it is "Romeo and Juliet.")

(AT RISE: we find the partially constructed set and we can hear hammering offstage. As the hammering continues, we hear a phone ringing. After several rings, we see VIOLET enter. She's carrying a clipboard and looks rather tired.)

VIOLET. Delbert? Luther? Ruthann? *(Pause as she looks as the phone continues to ring and the hammering continues.)* Will somebody get the phone, please? *(To herself.)* Where is everybody? *(She crosses to where the phone sits. Over the hammering.)* Hello? *(Louder.)* Hello? *(Louder, still.)* HELLO? *(VIOLET covers one of her ears so she can hear better.)* WHO? ... OH, YEAH, SURE HARRY. SHE'S HERE - JUST A SEC. HEY! YOU COMIN' TO THE SHOW? ... OH! OKAY. HERE - LET ME GO GET HER. HOLD ON. *(VIOLET crosses to behind a flat.)* MILDRED? TELEPHONE! IT'S HARRY! *(VIOLET turns away and starts to exit as we hear MILDRED from backstage.)*

MILDRED. *(From backstage.)* Good Lord ... like I have time to talk to him. *(MILDRED enters in the midst of "making-up." She crosses to the phone as she calls after VIOLET, who is exiting.)* Thank you, Violet, honey. *(Into the phone and still over the hammering.)* Hello? *(Louder.)* Hello? *(Louder.)* HELLO?!? *(Disgusted she slams the phone down and sticks her head backstage.)* DELBERT, WOULD YOU STOP THAT HAMMERIN', PLEASE? I'M ON THE PHONE!

DELBERT. *(From off stage. The hammering stops.)* Okie-dokie. *(MILDRED crosses back to the phone to resume her conversation.)*

MILDRED. *(Into the phone.)* Hello? ... Harry, what do you want now? I told you not to call me here at the theatre anymore. I'm busy! *(Pause.)* What do you mean "doin' what?" I'm gettin' ready for my performance. Now what do you want? *(Pause.)* Well, I don't know where the Fry Daddy is. Did you look in the cupboard next to the sink? Well, go look there and ... What? No, Harry! Harry? Don't put little Agnes on. Honey, don't put her ... Why hello there little Agnes sweetie. What're you doin', honeypot? *(DELBERT, from offstage, starts to hammer again.)* DELBERT, I AM STILL ON THE PHONE! *(Into the phone.)* What? No, I don't think you're brother looks like a frog. Where's your daddy, baby? Well, put him on, please. *(Pause.)* HARRY, I TOLD YOU NOT TO ... did you find it? Well, feed'em peanut butter sandwiches or somethin'. Harry, I do not have time for this. I've got to go get into my character, and ... hello? Oh, hi Bobby Lee ... no, sweetie, I don't think your sister looks like a tortoise. Let me talk to your daddy please ... NO I DO NOT WANT TO TALK TO THE DOG! Put your daddy on, please. *(Pause.)* Harry, what's all this talk about frogs and turtles? I think we're lettin' 'em watch way too much public television. Did you find it? ... Good. All you have to do is look. I gotta go. Don't let Bobby Lee have more than two corn dogs or he'll get gas. Bye. *(MILDRED hangs up.)* OKAY, DELBERT. I'M OFF THE PHONE, NOW. DID YOU GET MY BALCONY DONE?

DELBERT. *(Entering in overalls and a toolbelt weilding a hammer.)* What?

MILDRED. Did you get my balcony done?

DELBERT. What do you need a balcony for?

MILDRED. For the "balcony scene," you idiot. Now did you get it done?

DELBERT. Nope. I thought you could just use a ladder.

MILDRED. A ladder? Delbert, I am not about the deliver the balcony scene from "Romeo and Juliet," the most famous scene in theatrical history, sittin' on a ladder.

DELBERT. Mildred, I don't have time to build you a balcony.

MILDRED. *(Calling for VIOLET, who's offstage.)* VIOLET! *(To DELBERT.)* Well, we'll just see about that, mister! *(Toward offstage.)* VIOLET! *(To DELBERT.)* We'll just see what the director has to say about this! *(Toward offstage.)* VIOLET!

VIOLET. *(Entering, wearily.)* What, Mildred?

MILDRED. I need a balcony for my romantical scene and Delbert has refused to build it for me.

DELBERT. I didn't refuse.

VIOLET. Mildred, tonight's openin' night. Delbert doesn't have time to build you a balcony. Not on openin' night.

DELBERT. *(To VIOLET.)* I told her to just use that ladder she's been sittin' on. Don't you think that'd be alright?

MILDRED. No, it will not be alright. I told you already I am not sittin' on a ladder. *(To VIOLET.)* Violet, I don't mean to be difficult, but I'm not goin' on unless I have a balcony. A balcony is detrimental to the scene.

VIOLET. *(Wearily and hating herself for relenting.)* Delbert, do you think you could do somethin' like what Mildred wants?

DELBERT. *(Mumbling to himself as he starts off stage.)* Well, I'll try. I can't do everythin' 'round here. "Delbert, build the sets," "Delbert, do the program," "Delbert, make the popcorn ..."

VIOLET. Thank you, Delbert.

MILDRED. Yes, thank you, Delbert.

VIOLET. *(Calling after him.)* You've done a wonderful job on the set. We appreciate it. It looks real pretty.

DELBERT. Well, she's not done yet. I have a few more things to do. *(DELBERT pats a flat which falls over. Referring to flat.)* Like fixin' that right there.

MILDRED. AND buildin' my balcony.

VIOLET. *(To DELBERT.)* Did you get that scoreboard unplugged?

DELBERT. Oh, yeah! I'll get right on it.

VIOLET. Well, make sure you do. We don't want scores bein' given out in the middle of the show. I told the Council for Culture Recognition I didn't want to have the show in the middle school gym, but it's the only place available. So we'll just make do.

DELBERT. I'll go do it right now, Violet.

MILDRED. ... *after* you build my balcony! *(DELBERT glares at MILDRED as he exits back stage mumbling.)* Thank you, Violet, for takin' care of that balcony thing for me. I appreciate it.

VIOLET. *(Not meaning this.)* You're welcome.

MILDRED. Well, I gotta go get finished gettin' ready. Is Naomi here yet?

VIOLET. No.

MILDRED. Where *is* everybody?

VIOLET. I don't know. I gotta go check the props. *(VIOLET starts to exit.)*

MILDRED. Oh, and Violet?

VIOLET. Yes?

MILDRED. In case I don't see you later, as I plan on retirin' to my dressin' room in order to get into my character -- break a leg!

VIOLET. You, too, Mildred. And I mean that sincerely.

MILDRED. Yes, I know you do, honey. Oh, and just have my roses sent to my dressin' room.

VIOLET. Don't worry Mildred, if anythin' comes for you I know right where to stick it. *(The score board buzzes.)* I sure hope Delbert gets that turned off. *(VIOLET exits as MILDRED watches her go off. A door off stage slams and we hear a large dog barking. From off stage we hear ...)*

FAYE . *(From off stage.)* D.D., shut up! Down, boy! Down! Get down you dumb dog!

MILDRED. *(To FAYE off stage.)* Oh, hi, Faye. I was beginnin' to wonder if anybody else was gonna show up. *(Toward off stage as FAYE enters.)* VIOLET, FAYE'S HERE! *(FAYE looks at MILDRED then runs off stage crying as the door opens again and slams shut. RUTHANN enters carrying a clipboard.)*

RUTHANN. Good evening, Mildred. Whose dog is that?

MILDRED. *(Toward offstage.)* VIOLET, RUTHANN'S HERE! *(To RUTHANN.)* Faye's. Somethin's wrong with her.

RUTHANN. What, dear?

MILDRED. Faye. Somethin's wrong.

RUTHANN. Maybe it's something you said, dear. Did you say something to her?

MILDRED. Yeah.

RUTHANN. What?

MILDRED. Hi.

RUTHANN. Oh. Well, I don't think she should have brought her dog. *(Looking off stage.)* That thing certainly is ugly.

MILDRED. Mean, too. I hate that thing.

RUTHANN. And the theatre isn't any place for a dog.

MILDRED. Faye just ran back to the dressin' rooms without sayin' anythin' to me. It was *very* rude.

RUTHANN. I'm sure she's fine. Probably just a case of opening night jitters. She'll be alright. So, are you excited, Mildred?

MILDRED. I'll get more excited when Naomi gets here. All I lack is my makeup. And she's supposed to be doin' that for me. Where is she?

RUTHANN. *(Referring to her clipboard schedule.)* Oh, she'd better hurry. It won't be long until show time!

MILDRED. I drove by the Bee-Luv-Lee on my way here and it was shut up tighter than a drum. I just figured she came

AN EVENING OF CULTURE 15

up here. She was so excited 'bout bein' makeup chairman you would've thought someone had asked her to be First Lady. I'm gonna go check on my balcony. Excuse me. *(VIOLET enters with her clipboard.)*

VIOLET. Hi, Ruthann.

RUTHANN. Hi, dear. How are you?

VIOLET. Oh, alright, I guess. A little tired. Here are your community announcements. *(VIOLET hands RUTHANN the clipboard.)*

RUTHANN. Thank you, dear. Oh, there are a lot of them, aren't there?

VIOLET. Just read 'em off before the show begins.

RUTHANN. Fine.

MILDRED. *(From offstage.)* Delbert! You call that a balcony?!? It looks more like a pig pen. Do it over.

DELBERT. *(From offstage.)* Mildred, I don't have time to ...

MILDRED. *(From offstage.)* DO IT OVER! *(The dog starts barking as DELBERT'S hammer starts to hammer. To the dog.)* And you shut up!

VIOLET. *(To RUTHANN.)* Oh, no ... did Faye bring that dog?

RUTHANN. I'm afraid so, dear.

VIOLET. I hate that dog.

RUTHANN. We all do, dear. *(A door off stage opens and slams shut.)*

NAOMI. *(Off stage.)* Yoo-hoo.

RUTHANN. Here she is. *(Toward off stage.)* Mildred? Naomi's here, dear.

NAOMI. *(Running in, breathless, she enters dressed in a*

purple Antebellum dress complete with hoop skirt. A costume straight from the lawns of Tara. She's carrying a small, black sample case.) Howdy, y'all. Sorry I'm late. My car blew up.

RUTHANN. That's alright, dear.

MILDRED. *(Entering.)* Naomi, where have you been? I've been waitin' on you for a half-an-hour! I've gotta get my makeup done. *(Shouting.)* VIOLET, NAOMI's HERE! *(To NAOMI.)* Now, c'mon ... *(MILDRED starts to drag NAOMI offstage.)*

NAOMI. I said I was sorry, Mildred. My meetin' ran over time. You knew I had my meetin'. I told you I had my meetin'. And my car blew up.

MILDRED. What's that get-up you've got on? That's not your costume!

NAOMI. Oh, isn't this just precious? It's my Beauty Belle uniform. I didn't have time to change.

VIOLET. O.K., so now all we're missin' is Luther and Bubba. Naomi, do you know where Luther is?

NAOMI. Yeah, he had to go over to Bubba's to get his wrecker to tow my car. They'll be here as soon as they can.

VIOLET. *(To herself.)* I hope they hurry. *(To everyone.)* I'm gonna go call the "Gas 'n Go" and see if they're there. *(VIOLET exits as the score board buzzes and the dog starts barking.)*

RUTHANN. Naomi, I didn't know you were selling Beauty Belle Cosmetics! How exciting! Do you like it?

NAOMI. Yeah! Down at the Bee-Luv-Lee. I just love it! I'm just a regular little en-tre-pre-neur.

RUTHANN. And the uniforms are just darling! You look just precious. Cute as a bug's ear!

AN EVENING OF CULTURE 17

MILDRED. You look like Mardi Gras at Tara.

NAOMI. *(Ignoring MILDRED.)* Thank you, Ruthann. Well, like I said, I just came from my meetin'. It was so exhilaratin'! We meet twice a month down at the Howard Johnson's, y'know. Anyway, this mornin' we had Testimonial Time and you simply would not believe the effect bein' a Beauty Belle representative has had on our members!

RUTHANN. Really?

NAOMI. Marriages have been healed, health regained and one woman's eyesight was restored.

MILDRED. My, my, my, isn't that somethin'? Before you know it you'll be raisin' the dead with finger nail polish!

NAOMI. I always feel so inspired after Testimonial Time.

RUTHANN. Well, honey, you look just cute as a button!

NAOMI. And guess what I got this mornin'? An entire *new* line of Beauty Belle products that are simply wonderful. You're just gonna love 'em! *(NAOMI opens up her sample case.)* We've come out with an entire new line of excitin' colors guaranteed to bring out your best features! *(Showing some to RUTHANN and MILDRED.)* Aren't these just yummy?

RUTHANN. They certainly are pretty, Naomi.

NAOMI. Thank you. I thought I'd use these for our theatrical makeup purposes. So, who's first?

MILDRED. Me. I am. Let's get this show on the road. Now, make me look good.

NAOMI. Sit down here. *(MILDRED takes a seat as NAOMI prepares her makeup as DELBERT wanders on to measure for the balcony.)*

MILDRED. Now, don't give me one of those makeovers

like you did last month. What with all that Tropical-Gel Face Mask, Caribbean-luxe Body Cream and the Coconut Skin Emulsion you used, I felt like a mixed drink.

NAOMI. Oh, Mildred. You did not.

MILDRED. Now the character of Juliet is supposed to be young and beautiful, so make me look young and beautiful.

NAOMI. Mildred, I'm a cosmetologist, not a plastic surgeon. I'll do my best.

MILDRED. *(Viewing herself in a hand mirror.)* You got somethin' to fill in these lines with? You know, to smooth 'em out?

DELBERT. I got some wood putty.

MILDRED. DELBERT, DON'T YOU HAVE A BALCONY TO BUILD? *(The dog starts to bark. DELBERT lumbers off stage. FAYE barges into the room, still upset and shouts off stage.)*

FAYE. D.D., SHUT UP! *(The dog barks for a bit then quietens down. NAOMI continues to makeup MILDRED throughout the following dialogue.)* I hate that dog. Well, ya'll ... this is it. My life's over. I can't possibly go on tonight. Not after what I've endured today.

RUTHANN. Faye, honey ... what's wrong?

FAYE. Hi, Ruthann. Y'all, it's happened. What am I gonna do? I need to sit down. *(RUTHANN helps FAYE to a chair.)*

RUTHANN. Sugar, you look a little flushed.

FAYE. *(Sitting.)* I'm just a little shaken up. The shock, y'know. I'll be alright. I just need my friends around me right now.

MILDRED. When they get here Faye, we'll let you know.

RUTHANN. *(To FAYE.)* Faye, now what happened? Why you're shaking like a leaf!
FAYE. Oh, ya'll. This is really hard. My ... *(FAYE chokes up)* ... my boyfriend broke up with me this mornin'. *(FAYE breaks down.)*
RUTHANN. Oh, honey. I'm so sorry.
NAOMI. Your boyfriend?
FAYE. Yeah, Stinky. I've never been dumped before. I mean I've always been the dumper. I don't like bein' the dumpee. Y'know?
NAOMI. I didn't understand that, Faye. That's too deep for me.
MILDRED. Faye, I cannot believe you're upset 'bout losin' that loser. He was nothin' but trouble. I say good riddance to bad trash!
FAYE. He was a good man, Mildred. He loved me. He gave me stuff.
MILDRED. Yeah, he gave you stuff, alright. Stolen cars, switchblades and a necklace made out of human teeth! And Lord knows whose teeth they were! And he could've at least made them healthy teeth! He had to give you ugly teeth with fillin's in 'em.
NAOMI. That doesn't sound like a very glamourous accessory if you ask me. It's very difficult to compliment tooth jewlery. We learned that in comsmetology school. Chapter One.
MILDRED. He was a scary man, Faye. You're better off without him. *(To NAOMI.)* Naomi, what is this junk you're puttin' on my eyes? It stinks somethin' awful!
NAOMI. *(While applying the eyeshadow.)* Oh, this is

Beauty Belle's latest addition to their eyeshadow line. It's called "Ariba Senor."

RUTHANN. *(Impressed.)* Oh, how exotic!

MILDRED. It stinks! They ought to call it "Adios!"

NAOMI. It's a very special exotic concoction made by the native mountain women of Peru and includes four droplets of South American Peruvian Pigs Urine.

MILDRED. *(After a beat of reaction.)* Faye - I've got Peruvian Pigs Pee on my eyes. *(Beat.)* I feel so glamorous. *(From off stage a door opens and slams shut, the hammering begins again and the dog starts barking and FAYE immediately gets up and runs backstage.)*

FAYE. *(Off stage.)* D.D., you are drivin' me totally insane. If you don't shut up I'm gonna shave all that hair off you and make me a nice pair of gloves! Oh! Hey there, Delbert! *(And at the same time we hear LUTHER calling ...)*

LUTHER. Naomi, honey?!?

NAOMI. There's Luther! *(To MILDRED.)* There, Mildred, you're all done. Here's a mirror. *(She hands a mirror to MILDRED as she crosses to LUTHER who is entering with BUBBA behind him. Both look like they've just crawled out from under a car.)* Hey, there, sugar bear. *(She gives him a light peck on the cheek.)* Did you get my car?

LUTHER. Yeah, butterlips, and it doesn't look good, honey arms. It's at the "Lube and Tune." We came over in Bubba's wrecker.

BUBBA. Yeah. Luther drove 'cause all the way over here I was hangin' out the window shoutin' "Come see 'Romeo and Juliet'! Come see 'Romeo and Juliet'!"

MILDRED. Well that kind of advertisin' ought to pack 'em

AN EVENING OF CULTURE

in.

VIOLET. Well, I think we're all here. Right? *(Everyone looks around and agrees that everyone is indeed there. VIOLET crosses upstage and calls for FAYE and DELBERT.)* Faye, Delbert ... could y'all come out here, please. We need to have a cast meetin'. *(FAYE and DELBERT run out with DELBERT basically being chased by FAYE.)*

NAOMI. "Cast meetin'," it sounds so professional!

MILDRED. Naomi, shut up.

VIOLET. OK. Well, ya'll ... this is it! Are y'all ready?

ALL. No!

VIOLET. Oh, now, of course you are. We've all worked very hard and we're gonna have a great show. I just know it. *(BUBBA holds up his hand.)* Yes, Bubba?

BUBBA. I think we ought to do "Pygmalion."

MILDRED. Bubba, we are not doin' "Pygmalion." Now we've been through this a hundred times. We're doin' "Romeo and Juliet." It's openin' night. This isn't "Pygmalion."

NAOMI. Yeah, who'd wanna see a show about a pig anyway? *(BUBBA holds up his hand again.)*

VIOLET. Yes, Bubba?

BUBBA. Who am I playin'?

MILDRED. Bubba! You're Romeo!

BUBBA. Oh, okie-dokie.

VIOLET. Now, there are a few rough spots I'd like to work on before you get into your costumes, and ... *(LUTHER holds up his hand.)* Yes, Luther?

LUTHER. I don't have my costume.

MILDRED. Where is it?

VIOLET. Where is it?

LUTHER. At the house.

VIOLET. Well, you don't have time to go get it now. Ruthann, is there anythin' in costumes Luther can use?

RUTHANN. Yes, I think I can come up with something that'll do.

VIOLET. Thank you.

RUTHANN. My pleasure.

VIOLET. OK, ya'll ... I wanna run through the Prologue real quick. It's been givin' us problems. Y'all come on. Let's go. OK, this is the Prologue to Act one. Does everyone know where we are? *(BUBBA holds up his hand.)* Yes, Bubba?

BUBBA. In Mineola.

MILDRED. Bubba, shut up.

VIOLET. In the play, Bubba. Do you know where we are in the play?

BUBBA. Huh?

MILDRED. Bubba, just start at the beginnin', OK?

BUBBA. Okie-dokie.

VIOLET. OK, everybody ready? *(EVERYONE glances about then shake their head "yes.")* Annnndddd ... lights! *(During the following prologue, which is said together by the cast, no one is saying the same thing at the same time, making it impossible to understand.)*

ALL. Two households, both alike in dignity, In fair Verona, where we lay our scene, From ancient grudge break to new mutiny, Where civil blood makes civil hands unclean. From forth the fatal loins of these two foes A pair of star-crossed lovers take their life; Whose misadventured piteous overthrows Doth with their death bury their parents' strife.

AN EVENING OF CULTURE   23

The fearful passage of their death-marked love, And the continuance of their parents' rage, Which, but their children's end, naught could remove, Is now the two hours' traffic of our stage; The which if you with patient ears attend, What here shall miss, our toil shall strive to mend.

BUBBA. *(Being behind the others.)* ... shall strive to mend. *(Pause.)*

VIOLET. Well, that was better.

NAOMI. Well, I don't understand a word of it! What's this "where's civil blood makes civil hands unclean" stuff! I thought this was in medieval times. Not durin' the Civil War. If this play's supposed to be durin' the Civil War, where's Abraham Lincoln? *(BUBBA holds up his hand.)*

VIOLET. Yes, Bubba?

BUBBA. I'd like to play Abraham Lincoln, please.

MILDRED. *(Warningly.)* Bubba ...

VIOLET. *(Glancing at her watch.)* Well, we don't have time to work the other scene. Just remember that durin' Juliet's death scene to wait until she's dead before you come on, OK?   ALL. OK ... sure ... okie-dokie ... you got it, etc.

VIOLET. Any questions? *(BUBBA holds up his hand. MILDRED sees this.)*

MILDRED. *(Warningly).* Bubba ...

BUBBA. *(Sheepishly.)* Nothin' ... *(He takes his hand down.)*

VIOLET. After the performance tonight we'll be havin' a cast party at the Happy Heifer. *(Everyone reacts.)* You'll get a salad, steak and your choice of ice cream or fruit cup.

NAOMI. *(To MILDRED.)* I hate fruit cup.

VIOLET. Alright, then. I guess that's it. Break a leg everyone. Curtain in twenty minutes! *(The cast starts to disperse as VIOLET exits.)*

RUTHANN. Luther, you come with me and I'll get you all fixed up.

LUTHER. Thank you, Mrs. Barns. *(RUTHANN and LUTHER exits as MILDRED catches BUBBA. NAOMI is busy putting her makeup back in its case and exits. DELBERT turns back to working on the set as FAYE begins to stalk him.)*

MILDRED. *(Getting her keys.)* Bubba, could you please go out in my car and get my costume for me, please? Just bring it to my dressin' room suite.

BUBBA. Sure thing, *(Embarrassed.)* ... darlin'. *(BUBBA exit as MILDRED follows him out calling for VIOLET. DELBERT, still being closely watched by FAYE, starts to hammer.)*

MILDRED. *(Calling, exiting.)* VIOLET?!? *(The stage is now bare except for FAYE and a working DELBERT. FAYE, assumes her most flirtatious stance. DELBERT continues to hammer.)*

FAYE. Y'know, I just love a man who uses tools.

DELBERT. Huh?

FAYE. The sound of hammerin'. Ohhhh ... well, it just sends me.

DELBERT. Uh-huh ...

FAYE. Hey, have you heard the news?

DELBERT. Faye, I've been too busy tryin' to put this set together to watch the news.

FAYE. I mean the local news.

DELBERT. No.

FAYE. Well, let me just tell you, then. The headlines read "Faye McFaye Free." My boyfriend and I broke up, so I'm free to pursue ... other ... interests. Catch my drift?

DELBERT. Uh-huh.

FAYE. Didn't you hear me, Delbert. I'm free. I've never been free before. *(MILDRED, who has entered, followed by BUBBA carrying her costume, crosses right in front of FAYE and without stopping says ...)*

MILDRED. No, just cheap. *(MILDRED exits, followed by BUBBA, who stops and turns to DELBERT and FAYE.)*

BUBBA. I still think we ought to do "Pygmalion."

MILDRED. *(From off stage.)* BUBBA!?! *(BUBBA exits.)*

FAYE. Well, Delbert. I gotta go squeeze into my costume. Made it myself, y'know. Hope you like it.

DELBERT. Uh-huh.

FAYE. I'll be thinkin' 'bout you durin' the show. Break a leg! *(FAYE seductively exits with DELBERT watching. Across the stage a flat falls.)*

DELBERT. Dad gum it! *(The score board buzzes and the telephone rings and the dog starts to bark. The following dialogue happens all at once.)*

VIOLET. *(From off stage.)* Delbert, uplug that thing!

DELBERT. *(Angrily.)* OKIE-DOKIE!

VIOLET. *(Off stage.)* MILDRED, TELEPHONE?!?

FAYE. ALRIGHT, D.D., THAT'S IT! YOU'RE DEAD MEAT! *(MILDRED enters and crosses to the other side.)*

MILDRED. *(To DELBERT.)* Where's my balcony? *(She exits. Ad lib as needed until complete blackout. BLACKOUT. Curtains close.)*

END OF SCENE ONE

SCENE II

(SETTING: Later that evening at the performance of "Romeo and Juliet.")

(AT RISE: the stage curtains are closed and with a musical fanfare we hear ...)

BUBBA. *(From backstage and talking into the microphone.)* Is this thing on? *(Loudly into the microphone.)* TESTIN' ONE, TWO, THREE ...

MILDRED. *(Whom we can also hear over the microphone from backstage.)* Yes, Bubba, it's on.

BUBBA. *(To MILDRED.)* What? *(Once again into the microphone.)* TESTIN' ONE, TWO ...

MILDRED. Bubba, it's on. The people can hear you. Announce Ruthann.

BUBBA. Wh ...?

MILDRED. ANNOUNCE RUTHANN!

BUBBA. And now Ladies and Gentlemen, the President of the Mineola Society for Cultural Recognition, Mrs. Ruthann Barns. *(RUTHANN enters from stage right or from the center split in the curtain, if possible, amid the applause and musical fanfare. She is carrying a sheet of paper which is on a clipboard.)*

RUTHANN. Thank you, Mr. Bubba Bedford ...

BUBBA. *(From the backstage microphone.)* You're welcome.

MILDRED. *(From backstage, over the microphone.)* Bubba, give me that microphone. *(The following dialogue takes place backstage and we can hear every word due to the microphone. Poor RUTHANN remains onstage in front of the audience looking a bit uneasy, if not embarrassed, and more than irritated as the scene progresses.)*

BUBBA. Huh?

MILDRED. Give me the microphone! *(We hear the microphone drop to the floor.)* DON'T DROP IT, BUBBA! MY STARS, NOW YOU'VE PROBABLY BROKEN IT!

BUBBA. You should've caught it!

MILDRED. *(Calling.)* Delbert, come here and see if this microphone thing is still workin'. *(We hear DELBERT's footsteps coming up to the microphone.)*

DELBERT. What's wrong?

MILDRED. Bubba Butterfingers dropped the microphone announcin' Ruthann. Now it's probably broken. Check and see if it still works.

DELBERT. *(Directly into the microphone and very loudly.)* TESTIN' ONE, TWO, THREE ...

MILDRED. MY STARS DELBERT!?! DO YOU HAVE TO BE SO LOUD!?! *(RUTHANN, unable to stand it any longer, peeks her head backstage.)*

RUTHANN. Mildred, it's workin' fine.

MILDRED. Ruthann, what are you doin' back here? You're supposed to be makin' the curtain speech. Now get back out there!

RUTHANN. The microphone is workin' fine, dear. We can hear you *loud and clear*.

MILDRED. Oh, thank you. *(To BUBBA.)* Announce her again, Bubba.

BUBBA. Ladies and Gentlemen, the President of the

Mineola Society for Cultural Recognition, Mrs. Ruthann Barns. *(RUTHANN, humiliated, turns back to the audience forcing a smile, and as she does we hear from backstage ...)*

BUBBA. Here, Mildred, catch.

MILDRED. BUBBA, DON'T YOU THROW THAT MICRO ... *(The dog starts barking and the microphone hits the floor with a thud.)*

MILDRED. Faye, you come over hear and shut this stupid mutt up!

FAYE. D.D., baby, be quiet, sugar. Mildred, you know where there's any toliet paper? We're out. *(An adlibed fight breaks out between MILDRED, FAYE and BUBBA. The fight should carry on until RUTHANN runs backstage and cuts off the microphone. At that point the amplification of the fight stops, however we can still hear it from behind the curtain.)*

MILDRED. Bubba, you have got to to be the stupidest ... that's an expensive piece of audio equipment ... etc.

BUBBA. I thought you'd be ready to catch it this time ... etc. *(After RUTHANN turns off the microphone, she turns back to the audience and over the fight from behind the curtain she delivers the following dialogue. Please note that the fight going on backstage will need to be resolved rather quickly so the joke doesn't get old by playing too long.)*

RUTHANN. Good evening Ladies and Gentlemen and welcome to the Mineola Society for Cultural Recognition's Annual Fundraiser, "An Evening of Culture." *(Reading from her clipboard.)* I, Ruthann Barns, am your hostess, and this evening I will be leading you on a journey of merriment and wonder, as we depart on a magical melange of theatrical wonderment, travelling to the Shakespearean classics written by that bard of the Avon, Mr. Bill Shakespeare. Tonight you will be entertained by many of your favorite local citizens as they present to you that classic story of love, "Romeo and Juliet." But first, a few local announcements. *(She clears her throat.)* All of us need to remember in our thoughts and prayers Mr. Ernie Justice of Mineola. Mr. Justice was injured yesterday afternoon when his wife, Ethel, accidently hit his leg with the family weedeater. Mrs. Justice was gettin' ready to trim the sidewalk when Mr. Justice got in the way. He was immediately rushed to Franklin County Memorial Hospital in Esther Flats where he is listed in satisfactory condition. No charges are to be pressed against Mrs. Justice. *(RUTHANN looks down at her notes.)* And congratulations to our own little Miss Gertrude Brown, who's eight years old, for recently taking the title of Little Miss Petite Sweet Okra at the Pickler County Okra Festival. She also received ribbons for Miss Congeniality and Miss Talent, for which she tap danced while twirlin' a fire baton and singing a Loretta Lynn-Kenny Rogers medley. She'll be giving an encore of her talent this next Wednesday night at seven o'clock at the First Baptist Church here in Mineola. *(MILDRED pokes her head from behind the curtain.)*

MILDRED. Ruthann, would you please hurry up! *(MILDRED disappears behind the curtain.)*

RUTHANN. And now the Mineola Society for Cultural Recognition takes you back to the Middle Ages proudly presenting the timeless romance of "Romeo and Juliet" ... *(MILDRED, interrupting, pokes her head out between the curtains.)*

MILDRED. *(In a very loud stage whisper.)* STARRIN'

MILDRED HAYWORTH CARSON! *(MILDRED disappears behind the curtain.)*
RUTHANN. Starring Mildred Hayworth Carson and written by Mr. Bill Shakespeare with additional dialogue by Naomi Louise Farkle Carson.
NAOMI. *(Giggling from off stage.)* That's me.
MILDRED. Naomi, shut up.

(RUTHANN exits as the musical accompaniment swells and the curtains open to a dark set. The LIGHTS come up to reveal a very bad medieval set and a slovenly dressed company assembled on it. They stand together in a clump looking rather frightened except for FAYE who is flirting with the audience. MILDRED feels something behind her and discovers it's DELBERT still working on the set. He looks up and sees that the curtains are open and runs off. The remainder of the CAST just stands there not quite knowing what to do. LUTHER is dressed in remnants of incomplete costumes from storage. Perhaps big clown pants, bits and pieces of armour and a Santa Claus hat. Meanhile FAYE, who's playing the Nurse, has made her own very seductive variation of a traditional Nurses' uniform.)

VIOLET. *(Impatiently poking her head from around a flat.)* GO! Fanfare.
MILDRED. Huh?
VIOLET. Fanfare! Fanfare!
MILDRED. Oh, that's you, Bubba. Go on.

(BUBBA crosses downstage center and with a trumpet plays a very bad fanfare. When he is done he takes a quick bow and returns to the group. The following prologue is delivered exactly as it was before with everyone reciting at a different pace. MILDRED is over acting while BUBBA is pulling on his tights. MILDRED is the only one who knows this word-perfect, so delivers loud and clear.)

ALL. Two households, both alike in dignity, in fair Verona, where we lay our scene, from ancient grudge break to new mutiny, where civil blood ... *(Here NAOMI says ...)*

NAOMI. ... civil war . Oh, sorry ...

ALL. ... makes civil hands unclean. From forth the fatal loins of these two foes A pair of star-crossed lovers take their life; Whose misadventured piteous overthrows Doth with their death bury their parents' strife. The fearful passage of their death-marked love, And the continuance of their parents' rage, Which, but their children's end, naught could remove, Is now the two hours' traffic of our stage; The which if you with patient ears attend, What here shall miss, our toil shall strive to mend.

BUBBA. *(Still behind, as usual.)* ... shall strive to mend. *(The cast stands there smiling for a bit.)*

VIOLET. *(From back stage.)* Lights out!

DELBERT. Huh?

VIOLET. Lights out! Lights out! *(The LIGHTS go out and the scoreboard buzzes.)*

NAOMI. What's that?

VIOLET. *(To DELBERT.)* DELBERT GET THAT

SCOREBOARD UNPLUGGED! *(To the CAST.)* Get off stage!

MILDRED. C'mon, ya'll. Let's go.

(During the blackout we can hear the CAST ad-libbing their way off stage and we hear a CRUNCH! As the LIGHTS come back up we just see the cast exiting through the center arch, however since all of them have exited at the same time it's made a rather tight fit and part of the set has been taken with them. After the crunch we hear DELBERT ...)

DELBERT. *(Off stage.)* Dad burn it!

(The LIGHTS come back up. After a moment LUTHER, as Benvolio, enters in full medieval regalia. He trips. He is followed by BUBBA, as Romeo, he, too, trips. DELBERT suddenly appears with his hammer and nails down whatever tripped them. He then disappears.)

LUTHER. *(As Benvolio.)* Good morrow, cousin.

BUBBA. *(As Romeo. Pulling at his tights.)* Is the day so young? *(He gestures.)*

LUTHER. *(As Benvolio.)* But new struck nine.

BUBBA. *(As Romeo.)* Ay me! Sad hours seem long. Was that my father that went hence so fast? *(He gestures.)*

LUTHER. *(As Benvolio.)* It was. What sadness lengthens Romeo's hours?

BUBBA. *(As Romeo.)* Not havin' that which havin' makes them short. (*He gestures. From the side of the stage we see*

DELBERT, holding a tree in front of him to conceal him from the audience, edge across stage; his destination being the broken flat. During the following dialogue he takes a few steps at a time crossing to the flat.)

LUTHER. *(As Benvolio.)* In love? *(DELBERT takes a step and stops.)*

BUBBA. *(As Romeo.)* Out. *(He gestures.)*

LUTHER. *(As Benvolio.)* Of love? *(DELBERT takes a step and stops.)*

BUBBA. *(As Romeo.)* Out of her favor where I am in love. *(He gestures.)*

LUTHER. *(As Benvolio.)* Alas that love, so gentle in his view, should be so tyrannous and rough in proof! *(DELBERT takes a step and stops.)*

BUBBA. *(As Romeo. He takes a big breath and delivers the following quickly, all through which DELBERT is taking his steps.)* Alas that love, whose view is muffled still, should without eyes see pathways to his will! *(DELBERT takes a step and stops.)* Where shall we dine? O me! What fray was here? *(DELBERT takes a step and stops.)* Yet tell me not, for I have heard it all. Here's much to do with hate, but more with love. *(DELBERT takes a step and stops.)* Why then, O brawlin' love, O loving hate, O anything, of nothing first created! *(DELBERT arrives at the flat and still shielding himself with the tree, takes out his hammer and hammers through BUBBA'S next speech.)* O heavy lightness, serious vanity, misshapen chaos of well-seemin' forms, feather of lead, bright smoke, cold fire, sick health ... *(Having repaired the flat, DELBERT, still hidden by his handheld tree, simply crosses the stage in one continuous cross with edging as he did on the entrance.)* Still-wakin' sleep, that is not what it is! This love I feel I, that feel no love in this. Dost thou not laugh? *(He gestures.)*

LUTHER.   *(As Benvolio.)*   No, cos, I rather weep. Farewell.

BUBBA. *(As Romeo.)* Bye-bye.

(He gestures. LUTHER, as Benvolio, exits, center, and as he does so his sword, which is held before him, hits a nearby statue, which hits the floor with a thud. BUBBA stands there watching it fall. There is a pause with BUBBA still looking at the statue as VIOLET creeps on to upright the statue. BUBBA just watches her crawl on. She motions for BUBBA to get off stage. He looks at her, looks at the audience, then shuffles off as VIOLET creeps back off. Meanwhile, stage right, NAOMI, as Lady Capulet, enters followed by FAYE, as the Nurse. They enter, slamming the door behind them causing the whole set to shake.)

NAOMI. *(As Lady Capulet.)* Nurse, where's my daughter? Call her forth to me.

FAYE. *(As Nurse.)* Now, by my maidenhead at twelve year old, I bade her come. What, lamb! What, ladybird! God forbid, where's this girl? What, Juliet!

(This being MILDRED'S cue, she is supposed to enter through the door through which NAOMI and FAYE entered. However, FAYE and NAOMI slammed the door so hard that it's stuck. We hear MILDRED strug-

gling with the door for a bit with her adlibs underneath the struggle ...)

MILDRED. *(Off stage.)* My stars! *(The struggle stops for a moment and there's silence. Suddenly, to the left of the door, we see MILDRED'S arm punch through the flat, which is merely paper, and sliding through the hole she just made, she enters. As Juliet.)* How now? Who calls?

FAYE. *(As Nurse.)* Your mother.

MILDRED. *(As Juliet.)* Madam, I am here. What is your will?

NAOMI. *(As Lady Capulet.)* This is the matter - Nurse, give leave awhile; we must talk in secret. *(FAYE starts out through the door, but it's still stuck. She struggles with it for a moment, then exits through the hole made earlier by MILDRED.)*

NAOMI. *(As Lady Capulet.)* Ho, daughter! Cometh andth sitteth byeth meth. *(MILDRED and NAOMI together sit on a bench which is next to the wall of the house of Capulet. The bench gives way with a crash.)*

NAOMI AND MILDRED. Oh!

DELBERT. *(Off stage.)* Dad blast it! *(NAOMI and MILDRED, in "the show must go on" spirit, continue sitting on the broken bench throughout the following dialogue.)*

NAOMI. *(As Lady Capulet.)* Tell me, daughter Juliet, how stands your disposition to be married?

MILDRED. *(As Juliet.)* It is an honor that I dream not of.

NAOMI. *(As Lady Capulet.)* Well, think of marriage now. Younger than you, here in . . *(NAOMI points to the "Verona" banner.)*... Verona, ladies of esteem, are made already

AN EVENING OF CULTURE

mothers. The valiant Paris seeks you for his love. Speak briefly, can you like of Paris' love?

MILDRED. *(As Juliet.)* I'll look to like, if lookin' likin' move; but no more deep will I endart mine eye than your consent gives strength to make it fly. *(RUTHANN enters as a SERVANT through the ever widening hole in the flat.)*

RUTHANN. *(As Servant.)* Madam, the guests are come.

NAOMI. *(As Lady Capulet.)* Come, O daughter of mineth! We're off to a party so you canneth meeteth men.

MILDRED. *(As Juliet.)* Oketh! *(NAOMI and MILDRED struggle to their feet as the rest of the cast enters through the center arch.)*

NAOMI. *(As Lady Capulet.)* Welcome, gentlemen and ladies. You are welcome. Come, musicians, play. *(The music, which is of a medieval nature, starts to play and everyone starts to awkwardly dance with BUBBA being paired with MILDRED.)*

BUBBA. *(As Romeo.)* My lips, two blushing pilgrims, ready stand to smooth that rough touch with a tender kiss.

MILDRED. *(As Juliet.)* Then have my lips the sin that they have took.

BUBBA. *(As Romeo.)* Sin from they lips? O trespass sweetly urged! Give me my sin. *(BUBBA awkwardly kisses MILDRED.)*

MILDRED. *(As Juliet.)* You kiss by th' book. FAYE. *(As Nurse. Crossing to MILDRED.)* Madam, your mother craves a word with you.

BUBBA. *(As Romeo.)* What is her mother?

FAYE. *(As Nurse.)* Her mother is the lady of the house.

BUBBA. *(As Romeo.)* Is she a Capulet? O dear account!

My life is my foe's debt. *(MILDRED pulls FAYE downstage.)*

MILDRED. *(As Juliet.)* Come hither, nurse. What is yond gentleman?

FAYE. *(As Nurse.)* His name is Romeo, and a Montague, the only son of your great enemy!

MILDRED. *(As Juliet.)* My only love, spring from my only hate! Too early seen unkown, and known too late! Prodigious birth of love it is to me. That I must love my enemy.

FAYE. *(As Nurse.)* Anon, anon! Come, let's away; the strangers all are gone. *(Everyone adlibs as they exit. The LIGHTS go to black and there's a flurry of activity backstage, which we can hear although we can't see it. The dog starts barking again ...)*

FAYE. *(Off stage.)* Shut up, D.D. *(The LIGHTS come back up to catch MILDRED just coming out onto her balcony. She trips.)*

MILDRED. *(To herself.)* My stars! *(She adjusts herself and assumes her "Juliet Balcony Scene" pose. Meanwhile, DELBERT has crossed behind the arch from stage right to stage left and makes his way onto MILDRED'S balcony intent on repairing whatever made her trip. As Juliet.)* Romeo? Romeo? Wherefore art thou, Romeo? *(There is a pause as there is no sign of BUBBA, MILDRED's "Romeo." Louder.)* Romeo? *(Beat.)* Romeo? *(Beat. MILDRED exits out the balcony and screams backstage ...)* BUBBA, WOULD YOU GET YOUR BUTT OUT HERE?!? *(She re-enters and strikes her pose again.)*

BUBBA. *(From backstage.)* I ain't comin' out 'cause I look like a sissy.

MILDRED. *(As Juliet. Attempting to cover for BUBBA while*

edging her was offstage.) Oh, my dear Romeo, how thou doeth jest, you madcap medieval fooleth. *(She is now backstage from where we can hear ...)* Bubba, I do not have time for this nonsense! Now we've got a theatre full of people out there, and ...

BUBBA. *(Interrupting.)* I ain't goin' out there in this get up!

MILDRED. Bubba, you look fine. Now I have not sweated blood over this production to have you botch it up. Now come on!

BUBBA. No!

MILDRED. Bubba, if you don't get out there this instant, I'm gonna kill you. You understand me? *(MILDRED re-enters and once again strikes her pose.)*

MILDRED. *(As Juliet.)* Romeo? Romeo? Wherefore art thou, Romeo?

(There is a scuffle backstage as we see BUBBA. There's been a costume change from the first scene and BUBBA is now wearing, for some unkown reason, a Tutu. He is forced onstage by DELBERT. Once he is out, DELBERT runs back off and BUBBA stands there, centerstage and self-conciously pulls at his tights. There is a pause and we sense, correctly, that BUBBA has forgotten his lines. MILDRED, losing her patience and through clenched teeth, prompts.)

But soft, what light through yonder window breaks?

BUBBA. *(As Romeo. Loudly.)* BUT SOFT, WHAT LIGHT THROUGH YONDER WINDOW BREAKS?

MILDRED. It is the east and Juliet is the ... BUBBA YOU TOLD ME YOU MEMORIZED THESE LINES!

BUBBA. *(As Romeo.)* IT IS THE EAST AND JULIET IS THE BUBBA YOU TOLD ME YOU MEMORIZED THESE LINES!

MILDRED. *(Warningly.)* Bubba ...*(MILDRED advances toward BUBBA from the balcony threateningly. BUBBA fearfully cowers.)*

BUBBA. *(As Romeo. Sing-song.)* Would through the airy region stream so bright. That birds would sing and think it were not night. See ... *(He gestures up to the balcony.)* ... how she leans her cheek upon her hand! *(MILDRED, as on cue, turns to the audience with her hand on her rear end.)*

BUBBA. *(As Romeo.)* O, that I were a glove upon that hand, That I might touch that cheek!

MILDRED. *(As Juliet.)* Ay, me!

BUBBA. *(As Romeo.)* She speaks. *(BUBBA points up to MILDRED on her balcony.)*

MILDRED. *(As Juliet. Striking a melodramatic pose, she relishes this speech milking it for all it's worth. DELBERT starts to hammer.)* O Romeo, Romeo ... *(She notices DELBERT.)* Delbert, what are you doin'?

DELBERT. Fixin' this thing right here so's you won't trip on it again.

MILDRED. I am in the middle of my big scene, thank you. Now you quit that. *(We hear DELBERT mumble something inaudible to himself as MILDRED assumes her pose and starts her scene again. As Juliet.)* Romeo, Romeo, Wherefore art thou Romeo? Deny thy father and refuse thy name; Or, if thou wilt not, be but sworn my love, And I'll no longer be a

AN EVENING OF CULTURE

Copulate ... (*DELBERT crosses back to the other side of the stage behind the arch.*)

THE CAST. (*From backstage.*) CAPULET!

MILDRED. (*As Juliet.*) Capulet. (*MILDRED turns to cough. FAYE enters.*)

FAYE. (*As Nurse.*) Madam!

MILDRED. (*As Juliet.*) Nurse!

FAYE. (*As Nurse.*) Your lady mother is comin' to your chamber. The day is broke; be wary, look about. (*MILDRED and FAYE "look about" right, then left. MILDRED looks at FAYE, who is supposed to exit, but instead is peering out into the audience. FAYE spots someone she knows and sneaks in a small wave.*)

MILDRED. (*In an audible stage whisper.*) Faye, get out of here. (*FAYE glares at MILDRED, then exits. To BUBBA.*) Go on, Bubba.

BUBBA. (*As Romeo. Waving to MILDRED.*) Farewell, farewell! One kiss and I go.

MILDRED. (*As Juliet.*) Before thou goest, a souvenir for my loveth.

(*MILDRED takes a scarf and throws it down to BUBBA, which lands on his face covering his eyes. Through the scarf he blows his Juliet a kiss and begins to blindly stumble across stage as MILDRED is waving goodbye to him madly. Throughout the following dialogue, BUBBA continues to stumble across stage until he reaches a flat and crashes through it. He stumbles through with a crash and the dog starts barking.*)

NAOMI. (*As Lady Capulet. From offstage.*) Ho, daughter! Are you up?

DELBERT. (*Off stage.*) Dad gum doo!

MILDRED. (*As Juliet. To the audience.*) It is my lady mother. (*NAOMI, as Lady Capulet, sweeps onto the balcony.*)

(*As she enters NAOMI trips. MILDRED reacts as NAOMI recovers herself. We see DELBERT, through the arch, run behind the flats to stage left to repair NAOMI'S trip. He runs into FAYE who's running to stage right behind the flats.*)

DELBERT. (*Off stage.*) Watch where you're goin', Faye.

FAYE. (*Off stage.*) D.D., shut up! Quiet down, now! (*Meanwhile on stage ...*)

NAOMI. (*As Lady Capulet. She has no idea what this means.*) Why, how now, Juliet?

MILDRED. (*As Juliet.*) Madam, I am not well. (*MILDRED coughs. DELBERT sneaks on and quickly hammers then runs back across the stage, behind the flats, to the other side.*)

NAOMI. (*As Lady Capulet. This is NAOMI's "additional dialogue."*) Ho, daughter, you do not looketh well! Thou art as pale as the ghost of Hamlet's father. And I haveth just the solution for thine ailments.

MILDRED. (*As Juliet. Knowing what's coming up and hating it.*) You do?

NAOMI. (*As Lady Capulet. NAOMI whips out a small pink sample case which she snaps open revealing several small bottles, lip-sticks, compacts and perfumes.*) Thou needeth

Beauty Belle Beauty Products to give thyself a healthy look. Beauty Belle Beauty Products, available at the Bee-luv-lee Beauty Salon in downtown Mineola. (*She snaps the case shut and it quickly disappears as MILDRED stares at NAOMI dripping with disgust.*)

MILDRED. (*As Juliet. Getting back to the play.*) No, Madam mother, my heart is sick. Sick with love for Romeo!

NAOMI. (*As Lady Capulet.*) Romeo! Vie and hatred! (*NAOMI spits onto the floor.*) You must deny thy love!

MILDRED. (*As Juliet.*) Fair mother, I cannot. For if I cannot love him, I shall die! (*MILDRED and NAOMI stand for a moment, posed. VIOLET pokes her head out.*)

VIOLET. Curtain!

DELBERT. (*Coming out on stage.*) Huh?

VIOLET. Curtain! That's the end of the act! Close the curtains!

DELBERT. Oh. Okie-dokie. (*DELBERT exits and the curtains either close from the sides, or come down from above, haltingly. This takes sometime to accomplish. As the curtains begin to close, we hear ...*)

MILDRED. Well, *that* was a disaster.

NAOMI. I liked it!

(*All the while NAOMI and MILDRED are still onstage posed. Once the curtains are closed, and this is the actual intermission, we are able to hear the sounds of hammering, drilling and heavy set pieces being moved. We may also hear inaudible voices shouting orders, etc. The idea being that the cast is trying to repair the set damage done in Act One before the intermission is over.*

As always, the dog is barking.)

END OF ACT I

AN EVENING OF CULTURE

ACT II SCENE 1

(*SETTING: The Mineola Community Theatre, which is housed in the Mineola Magnet Middle School.*)

(*AT RISE: It is fifteen minutes later, after intermission of their production of "Romeo and Juliet." As the second act begins we hear ...*)

BUBBA. (*Using the microphone backstage.*) Ladies and gentlemen, Mrs. Ruthann Barns. (*RUTHANN enters in front of the curtain, behind which we can still hear work being done.*)

RUTHANN. Thank you, Mr. Bedford. (*To the audience.*) We certainly do hope you're enjoying this evening's performance of "Romeo and Juliet" and now, as a very special treat, our magical journey into the theatrical world of theatre continues as Mineola's very own poetress, that pixie of the pen and quill, Miss Faye McFaye ... (*FAYE runs out onstage and hands RUTHANN a slip of paper.*)

FAYE. Here, read this ... (*FAYE exits.*)

RUTHANN. (*Reading from the slip of paper.*) Miss McFaye, who is single, will be reciting an original composition entitled "An Ode to Tinkerbell. (*RUTHANN leads a round of polite applause as FAYE, dressed in a Pseudo-Tinkerbell costume, enters.*)

FAYE. Thank you, Mrs. Barns, for that lovely and sincere introduction. (*RUTHANN makes a slight acknowledgement, then disappears backstage. Addressing the audience.*) "An

AN EVENING OF CULTURE 47

Ode to Tinkerbell," by Miss Faye McFaye. (*FAYE coughs and adjusts herself. She raises her wand over her head and poses.*)

Tinkerbell, Tinkerbell, why do you look so blue?
Is it because Peter Pan is not in love with you?
Forget him, girl - he's just a boy,
A man he'll never be.
Do you wish to spend your life in love with pu-ber-ty?
But when she was alone,
She'd feel the heat of a love unmet.
So off to find her one true love,
One evening she did set.
Into the sky she did fly,
And her love she did discover,

(*FAYE begins to get emotional.*)

Locked into a warm embrace,
And in the arms of another.
The little sprite, she shook with rage,
And from her wand she did disperse,
As lightin' lit the nighttime sky,
She hexed them with a curse.
The moral is quite simple, dears,
Love is not a simple route.
For Peter Pan is now a she,
And Wendy's got the gout.

Thank you.

(RUTHANN enters leading tentative applause, unsure whether or not FAYE's recitation was worthy. FAYE, under the spell of the footlights, takes her bows while dabbing her tearfilled eyes.)

RUTHANN. Thank you, Faye. That was very interesting.
FAYE. Thank you, Mrs. Barns.
RUTHANN. And now, let us return to Verona and our story of classic love.

(RUTHANN exits as the curtain rises and we can still can hear hammering, nailing and drilling going on, and as the curtain rises we find DELBERT, unaware, still repairing the set. During the intermission the set has been "repaired" with masking tape holding the walls together and two-by-fours wedged to hold up what's left. After the curtain is all the way up DELBERT continues to work until he notices the audience staring at him. He then stops, and with hammer in hand, walks across the stage to exit looking at the audience all the way. Once he is off, we hear ...)

VIOLET. *(Off stage.)* Take the lights out.
DELBERT. *(Off stage.)* Huh?
VIOLET. *(Off stage.)* The lights! Take the lights out!
DELBERT. *(Off stage.)* Oh. Okie-dokie.

(The LIGHTS go to black and our cast, who have been waiting backstage, enter through the center arch. They nosily file on and gather in a clump center stage.)

MILDRED. Naomi, you're standin' on my dress.
NAOMI. Sorry.

(*The LIGHTS come up with the cast shielding their eyes from the sudden brightness. They stand in silence.*)

VIOLET. (*Poking her head out from behind a flat.*) Fanfare!
MILDRED. Huh?
VIOLET. Fanfare! Fanfare!
MILDRED. Oh, that's you again, Bubba. Go on.

(*BUBBA crosses downstage with his trumpet and plays another pathetic fanfare. The following dialogue is another chorus number which is delivered even worse than the one in the first act. In fact, the cast doesn't even get all the way through it, just mumbling and eventually growing tired of it and stopping, wandering off, except for MILDRED who sees it to the end.*)

ALL. (*During the following dialogue, as it progresses, the cast, one-by-one, wander off stage, leaving MILDRED, alone, to finish the chorus.*) Now old desire doth in his deathbed lie, and young affection gapes to be his heir; That fair for which love groaned for and could die, With tender Juliet matched, is now not fair. Now Romeo is beloved and loves again, Alike bewitched by the charm of looks; But to his foe supposed he must complain, and she steal love's sweet bait from fearful hooks. Being held a foe, he may not have access to breathe such vows as lovers use to swear, And she as much in love, her means much less to meet her new beloved anywhere; but passion lends them power, time means, to meet, temp'rin' extremities with extreme sweet. (*MILDRED stands for a moment, noticing that no one else is around her.*)

MILDRED. (*To herself.*) Good Lord.

VIOLET. (*Off stage.*) Lights! Take the lights out! SET CHANGE!

(*There is a black out for a "scene change." Everyone converges onstage enmasse attempting to speedily change the set for the next scene. There are general ad libs as set pieces are being dragged on and other pieces are being struck. We hear a loud crash. Everyone reacts.*)

MILDRED. Luther? You alright?

LUTHER. Yeah, I think so Mildred.

MILDRED. Faye, you go get somethin' to clean up the blood.

(*The LIGHTS come up prematurely catching the cast still arranging set pieces. Startled, they glance at the audience and race backstage exiting stage left. MILDRED remains onstage.*)

MILDRED. (*In a loud stage whisper.*) You're on the wrong side of the stage!

LUTHER. What?

MILDRED. You're on the wrong side of the stage! You gotta come in on the other side. (*There is a short pause, then*

AN EVENING OF CULTURE

everyone offstage, enmasse, begins to cross to the other side.) Not in front of the audience, you idiots! Go behind the set! (*There is general grumbling as the cast exits, with BUBBA following.*) Not you, Bubba. You stay here with me.

> (*The cast crosses to the other side behind the set. We are able to hear them adlib as they cross and we are also able to see them cross through the arch in the set.*)

Go on, Bubba. (*The following is NAOMI'S famous "additional dialogue."*)

BUBBA. (*As Romeo.*) Oh, Juliet. I love you. (*He gestures.*)
MILDRED. (*As Juliet.*) And I you, kind sir. But our love is forbidden.
BUBBA. (*As Romeo.*) Never fair, fear maiden. For I haveth a planeth. (*He gestures.*)
MILDRED. (*As Juliet.*) A planeth?
BUBBA. (*As Romeo.*) How we can have our love. (*He gestures.*)
MILDRED. (*As Juliet.*) Oh, I am as happy as King Lear's baby! (*MILDRED, disgusted, doesn't even wait for the light change, but instead strikes the chair in the light and exits.*)

> (*The LIGHTS go down to black. During the blackout, RUTHANN enters as The Friar. The following dialogue is played in the dark, due to slow light cues. There is a pause as BUBBA and RUTHANN are uncertain whether or not to start.*)

RUTHANN. (*As the Friar. In the dark.*) Who knocketh upon my door? Enter! (*There are three knocks.*)

BUBBA. (*As Romeo. In the dark.*) Good Friday Friar fair..

RUTHANN. (*As the Friar.*) What, ho, Romeo! (*Suddenly the LIGHTS blaze on, hurting the eyes of BUBBA and RUTHANN.*)

BUBBA. (*As Romeo. Shielding his eyes.*) How good it is to see you, Friar, ma'am. Do you haveth a planeth for me?

RUTHANN. (*As the Friar.*) Yes. The family tomb of Capucinno ...

ALL. (*From off stage.*) CAPULET!

RUTHANN. (*As the Friar.*) The family tomb of Capulet shall be the rendevous. There you shall find your Juliet.

BUBBA. (*As Romeo.*) Thank you.

RUTHANN. (*As the Friar.*) Don't mention it. (*BUBBA stands there for a moment, then remembers ...*)

BUBBA. (*As Romeo.*) See ya. (*BUBBA starts to exit.*)

VIOLET. (*From off stage.*) SET CHANGE!

(*The cast, still in the light, run on stage to set up Juliet's bedroom. Again, the light cues are slow and the LIGHTS come down as we see the bed being brought on.*)

TAKE THE LIGHTS OUT!

DELBERT. (*From off stage.*) Huh?

VIOLET. (*From off stage.*) LIGHTS OUT! LIGHTS OUT!

AN EVENING OF CULTURE

(DELBERT takes the LIGHTS out. However, by now the bed has been set and MILDRED, as Juliet, has taken her place. Just as she opens her mouth the LIGHTS go out.)

MILDRED. *(As Juliet)* Oh, what if it ... *(The LIGHTS go out!)* Hey!
VIOLET. *(From off stage.)* LIGHTS UP! LIGHTS UP! *(The LIGHTS come up.)*
MILDRED. *(As Juliet.)* What if it be a poison which the friar subtly hath minist'red to have me dead. Yeah, not really dead but a death of mere pretense. *(MILDRED dramatically holds up a vial filled with the potion.)* Yea, within this vial is a vile potion which shall give me but the semblance of death. And off to meet my Romeo I will be as we rendevous in the tomb of Catapult.
ALL. *(From off stage.)* CAPULET!

(MILDRED upstops the cork and dramatically drinks of the potion, falling onto her bed in a heap. NAOMI, as Lady Capulet, enters followed by FAYE as the Nurse.)

NAOMI. *(As Lady Capulet.)* Go waken Juliet; go and trim her up. Hie, make haste. Make haste I say! I say, make haste!

(FAYE crosses to where MILDRED is lying in a heap and lifts up her arm, which limply falls hitting the bed with a thud.)

MILDRED. Ouch, Faye. Be careful!

FAYE. (*As Nurse.*) Aaaaahhhhh!?!

NAOMI. (*As Lady Capulet.*) What noise is here?

FAYE. (*As Nurse.*) O lamentable day!

NAOMI. (*As Lady Capulet.*) What is the matter?

FAYE. (*As Nurse.*) Look, look! O heavy day!

NAOMI. (*As Lady Capulet.*) O me, O me! My child, my only life! Revive, look up, or I will die with thee! Help, help! Call help!

FAYE. (*As Nurse.*) She's dead, deceased; she's deader than a doornail, alack the day! She bought the farm.

NAOMI. (*As Lady Capulet.*) She's dead, she's dead, she's dead.

FAYE. (*As Nurse.*) O lamentable day. Whatever shall we do?

NAOMI. (*As Lady Capulet.*) Bury her.

(*The LIGHTS go out. We hear a mad scramble as the cast changes the set to that of the tomb. This is merely a bench upon which MILDRED, as Juliet, is to lie, and, perhaps, a tombstone here and there. When the LIGHTS come up, we find MILDRED lying in state. From offstage we hear a commotion and we can see the glow of a torch. Noisily LUTHER, as Benvolio, enters, he is wearing a bandage on his head and is followed by RUTHANN as the Page. RUTHANN is carrying the torch and a bunch of flowers. They enter and dramatically look about. They stop, pose and RUTHANN gives LUTHER the torch.*)

LUTHER. (*As Benvolio.*) Give me thy torch, boy. Hence, and stand aloof. (*RUTHANN gives LUTHER the flowers.*) Give me those flowers. Do as I bid thee, go.

RUTHANN. (*As the Page. Aside.*) I am almost afraid to stand alone here in the churchyard; yet I will adventure.

(*RUTHANN exits. LUTHER crosses down to where MILDRED lays and laments over her body.*)

LUTHER. (*As Benvolio.*) Sweet flower, with flowers thy bridal bed I strew. (*LUTHER throws the bouquet a MILDRED.*)

MILDRED. Ouch!

LUTHER. (*As Benvolio.*) Over thy dead body, dead Juliet, I must confess my love for thee and my hate for Romeo. (*RUTHANN appears and whistles.*) The boy gives warnin', something doth approach. What cursed foot wanders this way tonight to cross my true love's rite. What, with a torch? Muffle me, night, awhile. (*LUTHER throws the torch backstage and hides behind one of the tombstones. BUBBA, as Romeo, enters, with a sword, looking around. Suddenly LUTHER pops up.*) I do defy thy conjurations. And apprehend thee for a felon here.

BUBBA. (*As Romeo.*) Wilt thou provoke me? Then have at thee, boy! (*BUBBA draws his sword as LUTHER struggles with his.*)

RUTHANN. (*As the Page.*) O Lord, they fight! I will go call the watch. (*Thus begins the duel between LUTHER and BUBBA. They literally cover the entire stage with their fight swatting at everything, including the scenery, which they shred.*

They also fight over MILDRED, who, although supposedly dead, still cringes. Finally, BUBBA delivers the death blow to LUTHER as from back stage we can see smoke.)

LUTHER. (*As Benvolio.*) O, I am slain! If thou be merciful, open the tomb, lay me with Juliet.

(Through the arch, center, we see DELBERT run from stage left to stage right. Onstage, at the same time, LUTHER collapses and BUBBA turns to look at MILDRED. There is a pause as BUBBA has forgotten his lines. Through the arch center we see NAOMI, followed by VIOLET and RUTHANN, run from stage left to stage right.)

MILDRED. (*Prompting in a stage whisper.*) "Ah, dear Juliet, why art thou yet so fair?"
BUBBA. (*As Romeo.*) Ah, dear Juliet, why art thou yet so fair?

(Through the arch, center, we see DELBERT run from stage right to left carrying a fire extinguisher. We hear FAYE coughing and the dog starts to bark. In between coughs, FAYE is "ssshhhing" D.D.)

FAYE. (*Backstage.*) Ssssshhhh . . (*Cough, etc ...*)
MILDRED. Shall I believe that unsubstantial death is amorous? (*From backstage we hear the fire extinguisher going off and FAYE coughing louder and adlibbing lightly.*)
BUBBA. (*As Romeo.*)... that unsubstan ... (*Turning to MILDRED.*) Huh?

MILDRED. *(Raising up.)* THAT UNSUBSTANTIAL DEATH IS AMOROUS!

(Through the arch center we see NAOMI, RUTHANN and VIOLET cross stage left to right carrying pails of water. The coughing and the barking grow louder as the action on stage continues. We hear a splash and a scream. The following dialogue is on top of the continuing scene on stage. BUBBA and MILDRED continue as though nothing is happening.)

FAYE. *(Off stage.)* Aaaaahhhhhh!
NAOMI. Oh, Faye, sugar, I'm sorry.
FAYE. *(Off stage.)* I'm all wet!
NAOMI. *(Off stage.)* I was tryin' to put out the fire!
DELBERT. *(Off stage.)* THE DOG'S LOOSE!

(Everyone screams and runs from one side of the stage to the other, and we see them passing through the arch, center. During this we hear horrible barking and FAYE trying to calm D.D. down. We see her do this through the arch, too.)

FAYE. *(Off stage.)* D.D., calm down! Down D.D.! Down boy!
BUBBA. *(As Romeo.)* Yeah. Here's to my love. *(BUBBA takes his goblet and lifts it toward MILDRED as though offering a toast.)* O true apothecary! Thy drugs are quick. *(BUBBA takes a gulp.)* Thus with a kiss I die. *(BUBBA blows MILDRED a kiss, turns to the audience, then instantly*

collapses. RUTHANN, as the Friar, enters.)

RUTHANN. *(As the Friar.)* Romeo! O, pale! Ah, what an unkind hour is guilty of this lamentable change! The lady stirs! *(RUTHANN points to MILDRED as she suddenly pops up.)*

MILDRED. *(As Juliet.)* O comfortable friar! Where is my Romeo!

RUTHANN. *(As the Friar.)* Thy husband in thy bosom there lies dead. *(RUTHANN points to BUBBA.)*

MILDRED. *(As Juliet.)* Go, get thee hence, for I will not away. *(RUTHANN, having to supposedly exit at this point, has forgotten and simply stands there. MILDRED cues him again ... As Juliet cont'd.)* Go, get thee HENCE, for I will not away. *(RUTHANN doesn't budge.)* Ruthann, get off the stage.

RUTHANN. Yes, dear. *(RUTHANN exits.)*

NAOMI. *(As Lady Capulet. From offstage.)* Lead, boy. Which way?

MILDRED. *(As Juliet.)* Yea, noise? Then I'll be brief. O happy dagger! *(MILDRED stops as she looks for the dagger, which she is unable to locate having not been preset in its proper place. To herself.)* Oh, for the love of ... *(Disgusted, she starts offstage, her destination being an unseen prop table where she is to find the dagger. However, she's met midstage by FAYE who hands her the missing prop.)* Thank you, Faye. *(FAYE smiles and waves to someone in the audience. MILDRED crosses back and resumes the scene. As Juliet.)* O, happy dagger! This is thy sheath; there rust, and let me die. *(Much is made of this. MILDRED melodramatically lifts the dagger into the air and with a grand flourish, stabs herself. Thus begins a series of wretching noises as she convulses across the stage. Meanwhile, the rest of the cast is waiting at the arch center to enter, and as they start, MILDRED waves them off...*) Not yet ... not yet ... (*The cast sighs and once again exits as MILDRED continues her death rattle. From backstage we hear a phone ring as MILDRED continues to die. DELBERT pokes his head out from the arch.*)

DELBERT. Mildred. Telephone. (*MILDRED doesn't acknowledge that she's heard DELBERT, and continues to expire, however she weaves herself upstage, still dying and makes her way to the center arch. Once she gets center it's as if she's been healed and she runs offstage.*)

MILDRED. (*From backstage, and on the phone.*) Hello? ... Harry, what do you want? I am in the middle of a performance! I'm dying out there! ... What? I don't know where the garbage bags are. Check under the sink in the kitchen. Bye. (*We hear her hang up and then she lets out an enormous cry of pain as she stumbles back onstage still dying. She weaves center and with a great flair, she expires falling into a glamorous heap on the stage floor. There is a pause. To the cast backstage from her position on the floor.*) C'mon ya'll. I'm dead now.

(*Assured that the show can go on, the cast disappears behind a flat to wait for their cues as NAOMI, as Lady Capulet, enters sporting a Medieval "damsel in distress" cone hat, which is higher than the arch making it difficult for her to gracefully enter. Having made a first attempt at an entrance and failed by scrapping her cone on the arch, she positions herself sideways squatting down, carefully edges her way onstage, or, if the set is a breakaway, she can "bust through" the arch not noticing her mistake.*)

NAOMI. (*As Lady Capulet.*) O, look how my daughter bleeds. (*She has no idea what this means.*) O me, this sight of death is as a bell that warns my old age to a sepulchre.

(*DELBERT, as the Prince, RUTHANN, as the Friar, FAYE, as the Nurse, enter. FAYE, as the Nurse, sees the body of Romeo and rushes to his aide. Carrying her doctor's bag, she takes his temperature and checks his heartbeat with the stethescope which is hanging around her neck. As Lady Capulet.*)

Ah, Nurse, cometh and checketh upon my bleedin' daughter.

FAYE. (*As the Nurse. More concerned with Romeo than Juliet, she says offhandedly ...*) Ah, she be deadeth.

RUTHANN. (*As the Friar.*) See what a scourge is laid upon your hate, that heavens finds means to kill your joys with love. And I, for winking at your discords, too, have lost a brace of kinsman. All are punished.

NAOMI. (*As Lady Capulet.*) Ah, Nurse, give me thy hand. (*FAYE crosses to NAOMI to console her.*)

NAOMI. (*As Lady Capulet - Cont'd.*) I will raise her statue in pure gold.

RUTHANN. (*As the Friar.*) Go hence, to have more talk of these sad things; for never was a story of more woe than this of Juliet and her Romeo. (*The cast poses. There is a pause. A flat comes unhinged and falls.*)

VIOLET. (*From backstage.*) Lights out! Lights out!

DELBERT. (*Who is onstage.*) Huh? Oh! (*DELBERT runs*

backstage, the dog starts to bark wildly, the telephone begins to ring and as our cast begins to sway in their freeze, the curtain comes down haltingly, stopping and starting. Once the curtain is down we hear DELBERT, over the cacophany ...)
Mildred, telephone!

(The audience should, hopefully, be applauding madly. And when the curtains open back up for the bows we find DELBERT hammering away trying to repair the flat that just fell with VIOLET holding it in place for him. They are caught off guard, and not quite knowing quite what to do, take a self-conscious bow. Then one-by-one the cast comes on to take their respective bows forming a line across the center. When it comes time for MILDRED'S bow, the line should break in the center and form a "V" shape pointing toward MILDRED who enters to take her bow as though she just finished playing Medea. RUTHANN then steps out to make a few announcements.)

RUTHANN. Ladies and gentlemen, as President of the Mineola Society for Cultural Recognition, I'd like to thank you for your attendance this evening. Your support is greatly appreciated. We hope you to see you at our next production, in December, as the Mineola Society for Cultural Recognition proudly presents "A Streetcar Named Desire." And you are all invited to the cast party at the Happy Heifer Steakhouse. Thank you, and goodnight.

FAYE. *(Grabs the microphone.)* If anybody'd like a free dog, just see me backstage. And if anybody'd like to see me, you know where my trailer is.

MILDRED. For the love of ... Faye, this is the theatre, not the redlight district ...

(And they all adlib as they exit the stage and just as they clear, if you like, the balcony or another flat could fall.)

END OF PLAY

www.ingramcontent.com/pod-product-compliance
Lightning Source LLC
Chambersburg PA
CBHW052030290426
44112CB00014B/2451